KT-388-912

Exploring the
EXTREME

Keith West

Published in association with The Basic Skills Agency

Hodder & Stoughton
A MEMBER OF THE HODDER HEADLINE GROUP

Acknowledgements
Cover: Photodisc Collection

Photos: p. 9 © Hulton-Deutsch Collection/CORBIS; p. 14 © NASA; p. 17 © Fraser Barber/BBC; p. 21 © Alison Wright/CORBIS; p. 26 © CORBIS SYGMA.

Every effort has been made to trace copyright holders of material reproduced in this book. Any rights not acknowledged will be acknowledged in subsequent printings if notice is given to the publisher.

Orders: please contact Bookpoint Ltd, 130 Milton Park, Abingdon, Oxon OX14 4SB. Telephone (44) 01235 827720. Fax: (44) 01235 400454. Lines are open from 9.00–6.00, Monday to Saturday, with a 24 hour message answering service. You can also order through our website www.hodderheadline.co.uk

British Library Cataloguing in Publication Data
A catalogue record for this title is available from the British Library

ISBN 0 340 87309 4

First published 2003
Impression number   10 9 8 7 6 5 4 3 2 1
Year   2009 2008 2007 2206 2005 2004 2003

Copyright © Keith West 2003

All rights reserved. No part of this publication may be reproduced or transmitted in any form or by any means, electronic or mechanical, including photocopying, recording, or any information storage and retrieval system, without permission in writing from the publisher or under licence from the Copyright Licensing Agency Limited. Further details of such licences (for reprographic reproduction) may be obtained from the Copyright Licensing Agency Limited, of 90 Tottenham Court Road, London W1T 4LP.

Typeset by SX Composing DTP, Rayleigh, Essex.
Printed in Great Britain for Hodder & Stoughton Educational, a division of Hodder Headline, 338 Euston Road, London NW1 3BH by The Bath Press Ltd, Bath.

Contents

		Page
1	Marco Polo	1
2	Discovering Australia	4
3	Ernest Shackleton	8
4	Moon Landing	12
5	Michael Palin	16
6	Climbing Everest	19
7	Modern Explorers	24

1 Marco Polo

Why do people want to explore?
Is it because they want to know everything
about our planet?
Is it because they want to push themselves
to the limit?

Marco Polo was a very well known explorer.
He was born in 1254.
He was born in Venice, in Italy.
He travelled with his father and his uncle.
They travelled to China.
The Polo family were the first people
to travel so far.
Marco was only 17 years old when he started
his journey.

Marco Polo wrote down everything
he saw and heard.
He always carried water with him.
He also carried gifts.
The gifts were used to bribe
tribes and bandits.
He travelled with bodyguards.
Marco reached the Gobi Desert.
He knew the desert was dangerous.

He thought there were evil spirits
in the desert.
Sometimes the spirits called his name.
They wanted to take him away
from the path.
They wanted to separate him
from his family.
They wanted to kill him.

Marco met the Moguls.
Their kings were called Khan
Marco became a friend of the Khan.
A dead Khan was to be feared.
The Khans believed that those who saw
them die would be their servants
in the next world.

Marco saw the Chinese burn coal.
He thought their empire was the
strongest in the world.

When Marco returned to Venice
he wrote a book.
Marco wrote about people with dogs' heads.
He wrote about huge birds that dropped
elephants from the sky.

People did not believe him.
They called his work
the Book of a Million Lies.

Nowadays some people believe Marco
never travelled to China.
He failed to mention the Great Wall.
He did not mention Chinese writing
or chopsticks.

If people read a far-fetched tale
they call it a Marco Polo.

Was Marco Polo a great explorer
or a good writer?
You decide!

2 Discovering Australia

Not many people believed in a
land in the southern corner
of the world.
But some people believed.
They called the land Australia.

James Cook wanted to explore
the Pacific Ocean.
He set sail in a ship
called 'The Endeavour'.

Captain Cook knew he would
be away from England
for a long time.
He wanted his crew to stay healthy.
He made his crew eat fresh vegetables
and fresh fruit.

His crew drank orange
and lime juices.
They also ate pickled cabbage
and marmalade.

Captain Cook did not want
rats or lice on his ship.
He did not want creatures
that carried disease.

James Cook took scientists
and artists with him.
He wanted the scientists to
experiment with
new plants and animals.
He wanted the artists to draw
the new plants and animals.

His ship set sail from Plymouth.
The year was 1768.

The ship reached Tahiti.
The people of Tahiti made
Captain Cook welcome.
But they had never seen iron before.
They stole everything made from iron.

The ship sailed on.
It soon reached New Zealand.
Maori warriors lived in New Zealand.
They attacked the ship.
Captain Cook knew his crew were in danger.
He ordered his men to shoot.
Three warriors were killed.

The ship sailed to Australia.
The scientists discovered new plants.
The new plants were in one bay.
They named the bay 'Botany Bay'.

Aborigine warriors lived in Australia.
They attacked the ship.
They threw darts at the crew.
Captain Cook ordered the sailors
to move the ship out to sea.

'The Endeavour' got stuck.
It was stuck on the Great Barrier Reef.
If the ship was stuck for ever
the men would be stranded
in Australia until they died.
England was 12,000 miles away.

The sailors refloated the ship.

There were new germs and diseases
in Australia.
There were many creatures that could kill.
The ten most poisonous snakes
lived in Australia.

When they were in Australia 26 men
and four officers died.

Captain Cook set sail for England.
He arrived back in 1771.

But James Cook liked exploring.
He set sail for the South Seas again.

He called in at Hawaii to repair his ships.
The Chief made him welcome.
The Chief ordered his people to
feed the sailors.

Some of the crew argued
with the local people.
They argued about a stolen boat.
Captain Cook was involved.
He was stabbed and clubbed to death.
He died in 1779.

3 Ernest Shackleton

Ernest Shackleton liked to walk
over places no man
had been before.

Nobody had been to Antarctica.
He decided he wanted to go there.

Shackleton led an expedition
to the South Pole.
The year was 1908.
The expedition failed
because he did not use dogs.
Shackleton learned a lesson.
In future he would use dogs.

Shackleton wanted to cross
the Antarctic on foot.
He set sail from England in 1914.

Ernest Shackleton and crew on the *Nimrod*.

The ship was called
'The Endurance'.
The ship reached Antarctica,
but it became trapped in ice.

The ice melted and moved when the spring came.
'The Endurance' was crushed by ice.
The men abandoned ship.
They were trapped on the ice.

The crew had to walk 300 miles
on the ice.
They took lifeboats and dogs.
Then the food ran out.
They ate seal and penguin meat.
They also had to eat the dogs.

The small boats were launched.
The crew rowed to Elephant Island.
Some of the men had frozen feet.
The ship's doctor amputated their toes.

Nobody lived on Elephant Island.
If the men stayed there
they would all die.

Shackleton set sail again.
He had to find help.
He sailed 800 miles
across the world's most
dangerous sea.
He landed on South Georgia Island.
People worked on that island.
They rescued Shackleton.

The year was 1916.
The crew had been on ice
for almost two years.

They had survived in the
ice and cold of Antarctica.

4 Moon Landing

Have you ever gazed at the moon?
Dogs howl at the moon.
People have worshipped the moon.

Some people have wanted to explore the moon.

In the 1950s, Russian scientists
sent small animals into space.
The animals wore special pressure suits.
They were the first
Earth creatures in space.

Next the Russians sent a man into space.
The year was 1961.
The man was called Yuri Gagarin.
He used a parachute
to return to Earth.

The first American in space was called
Alan Shepard.

The Americans wanted to send
somebody to the moon.

Apollo 11 was launched on
11 July 1969.
It travelled through space
for three days.
There were three men on Apollo 11.
They were called Neil Armstrong,
Buzz Aldrin and Michael Collins.

Armstrong and Collins climbed onto
A landing module.
It was named Eagle.
Eagle landed on the moon.

Neil Armstrong was the first human
to walk on the moon.
'That's one small step for a man,
a giant leap for mankind,' he said.

Neil Armstrong took this photo of Buzz Aldrin after landing on the moon.

When the astronauts were back on Earth
they were kept away from everyone else.
They were alone for 18 days.
Scientists thought they might have
moon germs.

They were fine!

Unmanned spaceships have
been to Mars.
They have been to look
at other planets.
One day a manned
spacecraft might land
on an alien planet.

Would you like to be
an astronaut?
Would you like to walk
on an unexplored planet?
Who knows?
You might have the chance.

Future discoveries are out there.

5 Michael Palin

Michael Palin was an actor.
He always wanted to be an explorer.
He travelled around the world in 80 days.
His travels were on television.

Michael decided to travel from
the North Pole to the South Pole.
He started his journey in July 1991.

The pilot had to land the plane on ice.
He hoped the ice would not crack.
He tried to land the plane three times.
What if the ice was too thin?
The plane would sink into the Black Sea.

The plane landed on floating ice.
It was a scary moment –
one of many to come.

Michael Palin at the North Pole.

Michael went to Kiev.
He arrived five years after
the Chernobyl disaster.
Michael got close to Chernobyl.
He met an old lady
who would not move from the area.
She was too old.
There were ten thousand
children in the area.
Three thousand remain –
most are sick.

Michael did have some fun on his travels.
He was given a mud bath.

He travelled to Turkey
and was given a Turkish massage.

Michael arrived in Egypt.
He was told the curse of the
Egyptian tombs did not exist.
People who robbed the tombs
might have died from mosquito bites.

His team crossed Africa
and flew to South America.
From there he reached the South Pole.
He had travelled 23,000 miles.

His latest adventure was travelling in the
Sahara Desert.
He still wants to explore.
Sooner or later he will find
a new challenge.

6 Climbing Everest

Mount Everest is 29,000 feet high.
It is the highest mountain in the world.

In 1924 a British climber tried
to reach the top of Everest.
His name was Edward Norton.
He got close to the top.
He gave up because he was exhausted.
He also became snow-blind.
To go on would have meant death.

Two more members of the team tried
to climb to the top.
Their names were
George Mallory and Andrew Irvine.
They were seen climbing near the top.
Both men failed to return.
Nobody has seen them again.

They might have reached
the top of Everest.
Nobody will ever know.
There is no proof either way.
Their bodies are frozen
on the mountainside.

An explorer named Edmund Hilary
took part in many climbs.
He was from New Zealand.
He always wanted to climb Everest.
Hilary wanted to climb the highest
mountain in the world.

John Hunt organised an expedition.
Edmund Hilary joined the team.

On 29 May 1953 he made it to
the top of the mountain.
Sherpa Tensing also
got to the summit.
They were the first people to
climb Mount Everest.

Many people have
climbed Everest since 1953.
They have modern equipment.
They take different routes to the top.

Mount Everest.

On 9 May 1996 five different
groups all tried to climb
Everest at the same time.
The conditions seemed perfect.
Some of the climbers
had never tried
to climb so high before.

They wanted to climb to
26,000 feet.
They wanted to reach a place
the climbers call 'The Death Zone'.

The weather was cold there.
The temperatures were sub-zero.

A man from New Zealand
called Rob Hall was the guide.

Jon Krakauer was an
experienced climber.
He joined Rob Hall's team.
There were four other
people in the team.

They all climbed to the
top of Mount Everest.
Jon cleared the ice from
his oxygen mask.

The world lay beneath his feet.
He was standing on top of the world.
He felt good.
He was on top of the
highest mountain in the world.

He was so high up only a small amount
of oxygen was reaching his brain.
Suddenly a storm blew up.
It came without a warning.

Jon decided to climb down
Everest as quickly as possible.

His oxygen tank was almost empty.

He managed to climb down far
enough to get a new oxygen mask.

Then really bad weather moved in.
Six climbers had reached
the top that day.
Only two climbers survived.
Jon was one of the survivors.

Jon survived.
Many have died.

Even today Mount Everest
can claim lives.

9 Modern Explorers

Apart from exploring space
is there anything else to do?
Surely the answer is yes.

Modern explorers include women.

Ellen MacArthur wanted to become
the fastest British person to
sail around the world.

Ellen had always enjoyed sailing.
She was helped by her family.

She sailed around the coast of Britain.
Her boat was called 'Iduna'.

Ellen MacArthur took part in
the 'Round the World Globe Race'.
She sailed in a boat named 'Kingfisher'.
She had to sail alone for three months.
She had to face storms and cold icy seas.

Ellen also faced damage
to her boat and tiredness.
She could only sleep in snatches.
She was the only
person in the boat.
She could not let
the boat drift while she slept.

She was second when her boat
hit an object in the water.
It damaged the rudder.
Kingfisher slowed down.

Most people thought she would
overtake the leader.
They thought she would win the race.

Ellen refused to give up.

She almost won the race.
She came second.
Second in the toughest race in the world.

Ellen MacArthur on the *Vendee Globe*.

Ellen sailed into France on 11 February 2001.
She was the youngest person
to complete the race.
She was the fastest woman
to sail around the globe.
She was the fastest Briton
to sail around the globe.
She was only 24 years old.

Since then Ellen has taken part in the French
solo race called the 'Route du Rhum'.
It is a 3,540 mile transatlantic race.
She set sail on 10 November 2002.

She took modern equipment with her.
Some equipment was strapped to her arm.
It checked her sleep and
her skin moisture count.
It checked her stress levels.
She knew when she was overtired
and when she was run down.

She knew she would
meet 25 knot
headwinds and gales.
She had never been better prepared.

At one point she had not
slept for 36 hours.
Kingfisher was damaged in a storm.
But she was in the lead.

Friday 22 November 2002
will be a date Ellen will
always remember.
Her 60 foot yacht
Kingfisher sailed into port.
Ellen had won the 'Route du Rum'.
She won the race in record time.
She took 13 days 13 hours
and 47 minutes.

She was only 26 years old
when she became the first Briton
to win the single-handed race.

She said she could not
have given any more.
The race took every ounce
of mental and physical
energy she had.

But she had achieved a dream.

So there are challenges in
the twenty-first century.

What about you?
Are you up for it?